Unveiling Financial Secrets: Finding Lost Money in Your Books before and after the Pandemic

Vanessa Ann Bates

Copyright © 2024 **Van Bates Publishing**

All rights reserved. No part of this publication may be reproduced, distributed, or transmitted in any form or by any means, including photocopying, recording, or other electronic or mechanical methods, without the prior written permission of the publisher, except in the case of brief quotations embodied in critical reviews and certain other noncommercial uses permitted by copyright law. For permission requests, write to the publisher, addressed "Attention: Book Rights and Permission," at the address below.

Published in the United States of America

ISBN 978-1-963379-97-6 (SC)

Van Bates Publishing
1901 Amanda Ct,
Upper Marlboro, MD 20774
www.vanessabates.com

Order Information and Rights Permission:

Quantity sales. Special discounts might be available on quantity purchases by corporations, associations, and others. For details, contact the publisher at the address above.

For Book Rights Adaptation and other Rights Permission, Call us at toll-free 1-888-945-8513 or send us an email at admin@stellarliterary.com.

Contents

What Small Business Administration Says
About Business Failure 5

How Coronavirus Affects the Economy 8

The Pandemic That Stopped the Economy 11

Finding Lost Money 14

Profit-Loss Statement 16

How to Reconcile Bank Statements 17

Reconcile Book Balance 18

Balancing Statement to Get True Profit 21

Short Story 25

Companies Belly-up 28

Remembering the Bank Statement Is the True Profit
and Proves the Profit-Loss Statement 35

A Shortcut to Finding All the Lost Money Over
the Life of Your Businesses 36

Summary 37

About the Author 39

What Small Business Administration Says About Business Failure

Why does the Small Business Administration say that over half of the new small businesses will fail in the first five years and one third will fail in ten years? Not only the small ma-and-pa businesses, but the middle and large businesses are also suffering. It not only affects retail but all businesses in our economy. It causes a lack of jobs and places to purchase merchandise. It appears that all retail stores are going under, and we only have a few good stores except for the internet.

When stores go out of business, the economy suffers from income loss, unemployment, and services provided. This is detrimental to the economy. Nobody wants to lose their life savings or invest in a failing or crippling economy.

If the economy fails, there is no hope for tomorrow or the future. There has to be a major change in the way we think and process or do things or business. If the economy folds, there would be starvation, death, lack of life provision, and more. Your only hope is to look to Jesus Christ, our Lord, to resolve this crisis in the past and current pandemic.

The retail stores have been significantly affected along with a wide range of businesses including restaurants, service providers such as waste management companies, utility companies, medical facilities, and many others. As mentioned before, the retail sector has really gone under. There are only a few shops to purchase clothing asides the internet. The interpersonal relationship of shopping is lost, for example, fitting of clothes to your body size is lost. When you shop on the internet, you have to be precise in your fitting of clothes. After COVID-19, no sizing or trying on of clothes in stores anymore. You need to know your precise size. God forbid you gain a pound. At times, the dimensions of clothing vary among designers, with some designer sizes being smaller than standard sizes. How many jobs are lost because businesses fail? This affects not only the retail sector but all industries, including restaurants and many more. This happened before COVID-19.

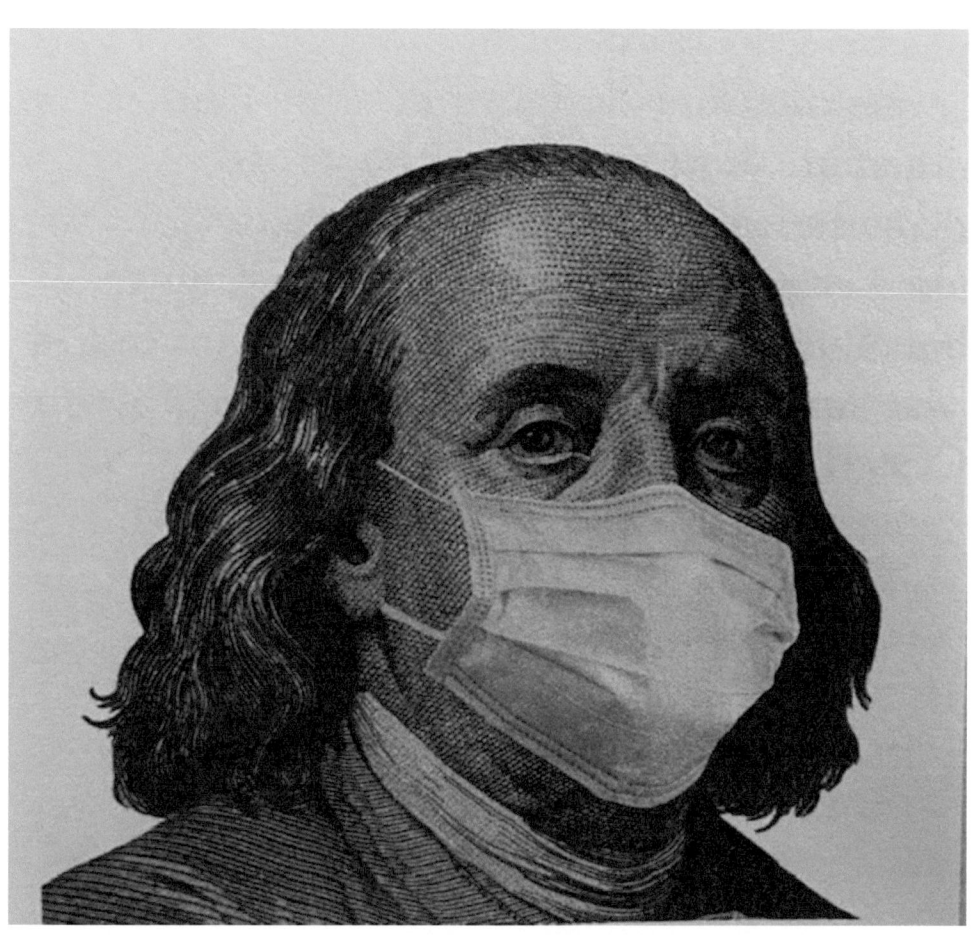

How Coronavirus Affects the Economy

Now that the economy is at a standstill with a loss of twenty million jobs, unemployment is greater than the Great Depression. Was this pandemic meant to not only cripple the economy financially but also to kill off all mankind? The private sector provides most of the income for the economy by collecting taxes from employees and paying one half of all American citizens' retirement program. If we get rid of the tax and write off depreciation to aid companies in their expenses, would it devastate the economy? How long will it be before the United States and the world economy go broke or collapse? Our only hope is that our Savior has someone to address the problem and rectify the error in the accounting system. I'm not saying this is the only challenge for failing businesses, but it is a major factor. COVID does not discriminate between race, gender, or age. It has killed over 400,000 United States citizens, constituting over 10% of the United States of America population. Worldwide, 95,000,000 people have caught the virus, and it has claimed the lives of 2,039,601 persons and the death toll keeps rising daily. DEVASTATING!! This pandemic has shut down the economy, closing just about all businesses.

In the era of the Great Depression, people queued in soup lines to sustain themselves. Now, people go to food banks to feed their families. Is history repeating itself? This pandemic causes death, not only poverty! We all can deal with not having financial stability, but when it comes to pain, suffering, and death, there is little hope!

How do we deal with a crippling economy? Businesses were failing before and after the COVID-19. As stated previously, over 50 percent of the small businesses fail in the first five years. Now that the coronavirus hit the world, all businesses have shut down. People have to keep a social distance of six feet from one another to stay alive. With its operations temporarily suspended, the government has transitioned to a socialist model by providing assistance to the citizens of the United States during this challenging period. The private industries, except for the companies essential to maintain life requirements.

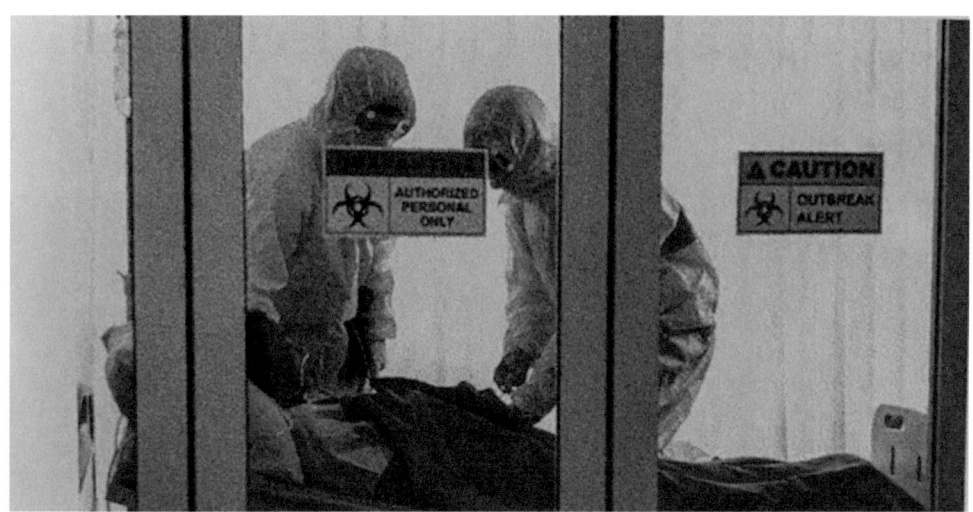

The Pandemic That Stopped the Economy

The impact of the coronavirus on the economy is very devastating. It has stopped and crippled the entire world economy. This is a latter-day plague the news calls a pandemic. This pandemic is worse than the Great Depression in 1933. During that time, only the United States, the most powerful nation in the world economy, collapsed. This illness or virus (whatever you call it), has hit every country in the world. It has affected the world with over a million deaths and also health-wise. Not only did it cause deaths, poor health, social distancing, and financial suffering; but it shut down the government and caused private industries to close businesses. It almost collapsed the economy. The United States government is signing a small business bill for the Small Business Administration to give companies that had to shut down or reduce hours of operation as a result of COVID-19. No one has money anymore. People are required by the governor's order to stay at home and either work remotely, or apply for unemployment benefits due to job losses. Only essential occupations are required to operate, such as sanitation workers, doctors, nurses, supermarket employees, and others. The government has allocated two trillion dollars through the Internal Revenue Service to aid people during this pandemic. The stimulus package, which is the aid money distributed to every eligible US citizen, including children, makes under $95,000 a year.

The streets look like a ghost town with hardly anyone on it except for essential workers or people who go to the grocery stores to get vital items necessary for sustaining life. There is a five-thousand-dollar penalty for entering public spaces without a face covering or mask.

It appears that before and after the pandemic, companies have been failing drastically, both major companies and small and medium-sized companies. Every industry, whether professional or non-professional is experiencing financial hardship. The sanitation workers, medical workers, retail or corporate industries, and entrepreneurs are wondering what went wrong with their businesses. Their profit-loss statement shows no income, and the bookkeeper says it's a paper loss. Hogwash! How can money be lost in paper? Laugh out loud! There is no such thing as a paper loss. It appears to me that the bookkeeping system never balanced the books, period! How can you have a bank balance and a book balance and they do not match or are inconsistent?

Finding Lost Money

What if I give you a little tip on how to find lost money in your books? Will this be enough to stabilize your business until this crippling economy recovers? You know depreciation is an imaginary expense – an absolute tax write-off. It is a momentum by the Internal Revenue Service for a tax write-off since the employer or business owner has to pay half of their employees' retirement taxes. This tax advantage was supposed to aid the companies to maintain the economy. Meaning, the retirement system for all citizens is financed by private industries or companies financing one half of each citizen's retirement.

All companies are responsible for their employees' retirement. If you are self-employed, you have to pay one half of your employee retirement. It is also known that most accountants do not deduct or expense the employers' half of the employees' social security tax. The information isn't noted anywhere except the 941-tax form. An over-sight! If not deducted the income statement is wrong. Could this be one of the reasons why Social Security is failing – not only Social Security but the entire economy? It not only affects the United States but the entire world. The depreciation tax write-off was to lift some of the financial burdens off the companies. The imaginary expense, tax write-off, and depreciation has to be fed, added back into the income statement or profit-loss revenue to rid the paper loss or imaginary expense. After you complete the trial balance and the profit-loss statement, you create a new statement and add all the depreciation back into the profit-loss or income statement. Reconcile bank statements and ensure they match the book balance. This will reveal the true profit on the Income Statement/ Profit-Loss Statement.

The trial balance and the reconciled bank statement should match. The profit-loss statement isn't exactly true until you add back the depreciation.

Profit-Loss Statement

Revenue							20,000.00
Depreciation Vehicle Expense	5,000.00						
Insurance Expense	10,000.00						
Insurance Expense	5,000.00						
Profit							0
Add depreciation vehicle back into revenue							5,000.00
Profit							5,000.00

How to add back the profits to recognize the profit in your financial statement

How to Reconcile Bank Statements

Look at bank statements: total deposits are your revenue for the month.

Cash

Less Outstanding Checks
Add Outstanding Deposit

Equal Amount Profit

Reconcile Book Balance

Look at your checkbook balance.
Check off every check to see if anything is still outstanding.
Check off all deposits also.
Subtract bank service charges from the book balance, such as return-check fees and wire transfer charges, etc.

Checkbook Balance

Balancing Statement to Get True Profit

The reconciled bank statement balance

The reconciled checkbook balance

The profit-loss statement after depreciation is added back in

The balances of all three statements above should align.

This is how you reconcile your bank statements:

You take your book balance of the bank statement or your checking account book and subtract any bank charges, such as return charges and account charges. Then, you take the bank statement and add in all outstanding deposits and deduct or subtract outstanding checks from the account balance. After your complete reconciliation of the bank statement, you match it with the book balance to reveal the true profit in the Income Statement /Profit-Loss Statement. This eliminates double counting; you deduct the note expense and depreciate the asset. The two balances should match up, and don't forget your prepaid expenses. You should find the money in your bank account.

If you have one thousand dollars depreciation from your profit-loss statement, that money is still in your account because it's an imaginary expense. You never spent that money. Therefore, all the depreciation expense is hidden in your bank account. If you cannot find the money in your bank account, where did the money go? Check with your accountant or bank to find the lost money, especially if you only spent your revenue by your profit-loss statement, and you suffered a paper loss. If it goes further, check with the United States office of Federal Reserve that houses all the bank accounts and their revenue. The Federal Reserve controls the banks.

If you find that the money is missing, check with the accountants also. There is always a paper trail of where money went. Check to see if any large checks were withdrawn from your account. If so, the security department of the bank can access the account from which the funds were withdrawn and put the funds back into your account as long as you have proof.

The money is in the bank accounts. The business owners and the accountants are unaware of this misappropriated fund because this has been an accountant error for years. I was looking for logical answers, such as, what's a paper loss? This is a good business, why isn't there a profit? Why is there money in an account but not on books? You need to keep records, and a simple correction of one accounting procedure will enhance your business and books, revealing the true profit-loss of your company.

I can give you advice on how to rectify the problem, but it takes God, the Superior Authority and Power, to turn a curse into a blessing. Seek the Lord in all things you do. Not pointing the finger at any one, accountants, or financial institutions may suspect fraud because they really don't know. This procedure was never used before from the beginning of time to the present day. The books were never accurate until 1994 when the cash analysis statement was implemented. Hopefully, this will help the economy and help you find lost money in your books. The analysis should show the accurate bank account balance. Adding depreciation back in the profit-loss statement or the income statement shows the true profit. I just realized this problem with the bookkeeping system and figured out what the problem is and how to correct the problem.

Therefore, do not fault your accountants, or your financial institutions unless there is a foul play, or proof of theft because it's an error, whether honest or not. The accountants are to prepare your books according to the standards set by the Principal Accountant Office which adheres to a code of ethics. They never knew that depreciation had to be fed back into the profit-loss statement cash balance and should align with the bank statement. The bank balance, after you reconcile your bank statement, is really accurate. You have to prove it with your book balance. If they are unable to locate your money, contact the security department of the bank for misappropriated funds.

HOPEFULLY, THIS WILL HELP THE ECONOMY AND HELP YOU FIND LOST MONEY IN YOUR BOOKS!

Short Story

Once upon a time, in a bustling town filled with small and medium businesses, there was a sense of excitement and prosperity. People enjoyed strolling through the streets, admiring the shops, and supporting their local entrepreneurs. However, the dawning of the coronavirus pandemic brought about unexpected challenges that no one could have anticipated.

As the virus spread rapidly, businesses were forced to shut their doors temporarily. The months turned into a year, causing countless small and medium enterprises to suffer severe financial setbacks. Many were unable to survive the economic strain and reluctantly filed for bankruptcy.

One common theme emerged amongst these struggling businesses: the challenge of properly accounting for depreciation costs. While depreciation costs did represent the decrease in value of their assets over time, it also provided entrepreneurs with several advantages. However, a lack of understanding and miscalculations of financial statements led to confusion and financial turmoil.

In the midst of this chaos, an accounting advisor named Samuel arrived in town. Hearing about the dire state of affairs, Samuel took it upon himself to share his expertise and enlighten the desperate business owners about the true impact of depreciation costs.

Samuel explained that while depreciation cost affected the value of assets on paper, it also allowed entrepreneurs to acquire assets at a lower cost over time. Additionally, he highlighted the advantages of properly accounting for depreciation costs, including the ability to deduct them from taxable income and the potential to use them to secure financing.

Gathered in a worn-down community center, the concerned business owners listened attentively as Samuel presented his unique perspective. He acknowledged that proper depreciation accounting was essential in accurately reflecting the financial health of a business but also emphasized its potential benefits.

Inspired by Samuel's explanations, the business owners began to reevaluate their financial statements and correct their depreciation calculations. They realized that by accurately accounting for depreciation, they could showcase the true value of their assets and leverage them effectively for financial growth.

Furthermore, Samuel encouraged the entrepreneurs to explore additional revenue streams, just as he had previously advised. He highlighted the importance of investing in new technologies and diversifying their business models to adapt to changing customer needs. By doing so, they would not only stay afloat during challenging times but also create new opportunities for growth.

The advice sparked a renewed sense of hope and determination among the struggling entrepreneurs. They eagerly embraced Samuel's guidance and embarked upon revitalizing their businesses. They sought to attract new customers through innovative marketing strategies, ventured into online platforms, and forged partnerships to increase their market reach. Months passed, and the town began to experience a revival. Small and medium businesses reopened their doors, armed with both a better understanding of depreciation costs and a newfound resilience. With the careful implementation of Samuel's advice, many entrepreneurs managed to overcome their financial challenges and gradually transform their businesses into thriving enterprises.

The legacy of Samuel's unique perspective on depreciation costs lingered in the town long after his departure. The business community developed a stronger financial acumen, allowing them to navigate future economic uncertainties and adapt to changing circumstances. Entrepreneurs began to see depreciation as more than a burden and recognized its potential benefits for their business growth.

And so, the small and medium businesses not only survived the pandemic but thrived, thanks to their ability to understand the true impact of depreciation costs and the invaluable advice bestowed upon them by Samuel. They emerged stronger, more resilient, and equipped to seize opportunities and overcome challenges on their journey towards success.

Companies Belly-up

There would be no need for companies to belly-up under five years, as the accountant said. No one came up with this solution before. Was it an intentional or unintentional over-sight? Did you find the money in your bank account, or did you sell the business and incur a loss of profit? The profit would be in your closed bank accounts. I am not saying that was the only, but one of the reasons why businesses go out of business.

We are not going to say this is a fraudulent or criminal act because this technique was never used before. I discovered it when I was suffering paper losses and knew there was money somewhere in the company. The accountants could not help because they went by the accountants' principle and never taught or discovered this concept. I always think outside the box but within the law.

Questions: Why is there extra money in the bank? How do we get rid of paper loss? Why are businesses going out in five years? Does this affect all industries – is this principle world-wide? Will this help all mankind and boost the economy for more people to become profitable business owners? Would the economy fail because of so many businesses failing and the loss of jobs? Could this simple technique save mankind throughout the world? Would this be a simple step for all accountants anywhere to use?

I am not saying there is no need for accountants because every company needs to keep records, but the old method was not proficient enough to keep businesses afloat. No one knew this prior to 1987 and 1994. Then, they executed the cash-flow statement. This statement was supposed to tell where the profit went – either reinvested in the company's business operation expenses, finances, or investments.

Adding back depreciation into the profit-loss statement gives the true profit for the stated period. The cash-flow analysis statement gives the true balance in the bank account. If depreciation is not added back and employers' half of social security are not deducted, the income statement and the cash flow analysis would be incorrect. Make adjustments, and see if you cannot find the money. Then, add the balance of the cash-flow analysis to the previous month's bank statements, and the figures should match. You can always reconcile bank statements to match. This procedure with cost accounting business should be bursting in profit, and the economy should be better than ever before. Also, the records would be more accurate. More people would be investing in businesses and making more jobs available for the masses. I want to reiterate that this is not the only cause of business failure, but it does contribute towards it.

Were this part of the stock market crashes in the '90s? Companies depreciate their assets and have a paper loss going by the income statement, not realizing there was revenue in the bank. Some car companies went out of business, while other companies' stock reduced, some as low as ten cents a share. This is speculative, but could this have contributed to the failure of businesses, such as car companies, at the turn of the century? Unless this procedure is corrected, will history repeat itself? We have to prevent history from repeating itself. Would we be able to make a turn around like we did in the turn of the twenty-first century?

Anyone that had a lot of assets to depreciate for tax savings would have a lot of income left in their bank account. If for some reason, the accountant did not know this and wrote a paper loss, this would be detrimental to the company or corporation. No one knew of this procedure at the turn of the century because I just developed it within the last five years. I have been trying to tell the accountants and public of my findings, but they do not think it's feasible. Therefore, I decided to write this book explaining my findings, so as to help mankind.

The coronavirus has most businesses at a standstill with no money and lost revenue. The world economy is affected, with over 2,039,601 people dead from the virus. The restaurants suffer the hardest hit, with the government and private sectors shut down. The nursing homes, assisted living facilities, and other hospital facilities are under lockdown. The restaurants have gone out of business, carrying out only. Social events are canceled, and only ten people can be together at one time. What will become of our economy? The citizens of the United States of America may have to stay at home for a month collecting unemployment and federal government grants to help through these hard times of lack of income.

Different countries have provided aid and assistance for combating the coronavirus. The government is giving two trillion dollars in payments to support United States citizens who are unable to work during this period of tribulations, ensuring their survival. People are unable to pay bills like mortgage and rent. Some states are helping while others defer evictions. Will this pandemic cripple the economy worldwide? Some countries have authorized their law enforcement to shoot anyone that becomes ill with the virus. WHERE DID LOVE AND COMPASSION GO?

Change! People do not like change. They get accustomed to doing things the way of the past, especially the older generation. One example is when the computer came into the picture. The older generation retired rather than learn a new method of processing work. You have to teach people, more or less in this situation, the accountants, my new method to enhance the economy. They have to be taught how to amend the error that has gone on for so many years. If this problem is not corrected, the economy will fold alongside the business.

One example is when recycling started, prompting me to open a recycling company. The government paid us to deliver recycling buckets to homeowners. My brother noticed that on every street he placed buckets, they were missing or disappearing. He finally caught up with the person and asked excitedly, "What are you doing with our recycling buckets? We are trying to help save the environment." The man said, "I have real good laundry baskets." My brother said, "No, we are trying to save the environment." The man pulled his fist back and said, "Didn't I tell you I have nice laundry baskets?" My brother said, "You have some real nice laundry baskets." I am telling you, change has to be explained and taught, including why the previous way didn't work and how to rectify the problem. Once the problem is corrected, businesses and the economy will thrive again. The need for public assistance, Medicare, welfare, SSI, and social assistance programs should decrease along with unemployment.

Some of the world's problems can be addressed, such as seniors in nursing homes having to give all their retirement income to the facility and being left with approximately one dollar a day to live on. Seniors have to decide on whether to take costly medicine for pain or eat cat food, or wear old-fashioned clothes because of no income.

The family can't help because they are strapped for money. The high cost of housing and childcare almost rival a mortgage which cost $1,200 a month, and rent, $2,000 or more. You're faced with living with someone or marrying in order to survive. The average single person's income is around $2,000 a month. You really don't have money for other expenses like transportation, car insurance, or even to help grandma and grandpa in a nursing home. The grandkids are stuck with a student loan that takes them almost twenty years to repay, not allowing them to invest in a home.

Everyone is suffering. God forbid if someone gets sick due to the high cost of health insurance, and this doesn't cover you if you're pregnant. The person has to pay an average of $40,000 to have a baby. If they don't have the money saved and have to get on Medicaid, they have to give up all their world assets, including their insurance policies. The government is supposed to be for the people, by the people, of the people, and not to destroy the people. Everyone at one point in their lives may need a helping hand and this should not cost them their livelihood.

AGAIN, EVERYONE IS SUFFERING FROM DIAPERS TO DEPENDS!! Once the bookkeeping problem is rectified, some of the above issues can be addressed.

Remembering the Bank Statement Is the True Profit and Proves the Profit-Loss Statement

Therefore, I am reiterating that when you process your trial balance, all depreciation taken from the income statement or the profit-loss statement must be added back into the income since it is an imaginary expense. The depreciation expense was never deducted from your cash account. Therefore, I have come up with the conclusion that your bank statement balance should agree with your book balance. The two figures should align.

Remember to deduct employers' share of social security, and when you do the cash analysis, include depreciation in operating expenses and deduct any financial investments to get the true bank balance. If you don't do this, the books will be wrong and can't determine the true profit of books. Trust the reconciled bank statement.

Remember to reconcile your bank statement, as previously explained in this book. Hopefully, this information will save the economy and have businesses and jobs bursting in profit again. God loves you and wants you to be a good steward over your blessings. Find your lost money! Look in your closed bank accounts, the bank, or check with the security department of your bank if your books show there was a profit not accounted for when you were in business or your current business.

A Shortcut to Finding All the Lost Money Over the Life of Your Businesses

A shortcut of finding all the depreciation over the years to add back into cash is to look at your balance sheet. Under each asset is accumulated depreciation. This is your lost money that you can find in your bank accounts. It doesn't show as cash; instead, it reduces the value of the asset. Once you gather all the accumulated depreciation over the years, you will find lost money that should be in your bank account.

 Maybe you can find enough money to stabilize your company that you don't have to close. The bible says three bear witness. The income statement, the balance sheet and your bank statement all show income. This is how you find lost money in your accounts. Confirm the lost money with the bank account balance and you'll discover all through the years, the Accumulated Depreciation and the tax write-off never left your bank account. Or you can add each profit-loss statement individually back to get each month's lost income, then go back through the years. Make it easy on yourself to take the information from your balance sheet over the years or life of the assets. For example, if you have a building cost of $400,000 fully depreciated, Machinery $100,000, Trucks $50,000, then $550,000 is in your bank account if you only spent money by your financial statements. Lol, you're in the money! Be blessed according to God's will, pressed down, shaken together, and running over.

Summary

The coronavirus has killed over 400,000 United States of America citizens, that is over 10% of the United States population. Worldwide 95,000,000 people have caught the virus, and it has claimed the lives of 2,039,601 persons and the death toll is rising.

So much has happened since I began writing this book. The administration has been helpful to the public, first with the $1,200 stimulus check, and now with $600 and possibly an additional $2,000. The citizens are suffering with over 94 million people not working. Most people are five months behind in their rent or mortgage. It used to be people living from paycheck to paycheck. The coronavirus has closed most of the businesses, and the people are practicing social distance because the virus has killed over 330,000 United States citizens, more than 10% of the United States of America population. More than 33% of the middle-class citizens are now at poverty level. Unemployment benefits cannot sustain the citizens that are now jobless.

Children attend virtual schools and the ones that don't have a Wi-Fi have to go to the public library or McDonalds or stores that have a free Wi-Fi to do their school work. With the schools' temporary closure, the children that get free lunch and breakfast are without any food. Therefore, more soup kitchens and food banks are established. Over 35% of the people have put college on hold because most of them are virtual. You teach yourself online, and they have to worry about staying safe and human survival. There are grants and loans for some of the businesses that are suffering or had to close because of the pandemic. The restaurants, sporting centers, movies, organizations or meetings, and many more that require large crowds are suspended. Will the old way of life return once the pandemic is over?

I suggested spraying the atmosphere to eradicate the COVID-19 virus, starting from the United States and then spreading globally. Do you remember when the earth was sprayed to control pests like mosquitoes and for crop dusting? Let's disinfect for the COVID-19 with Lysol or Microban. Along with the vaccination, we should be okay. The bible says faith without works is dead. You do a little something and God gives the increase.

The people demonstrate love and compassion for the hurting and needy by giving unemployment benefits, supporting food banks and issuing stimulus checks. This is so helpful but not the answer to the problems. The solution is to eliminate the COVID-19 virus and address the underlying issue causing the closure of stores and industries, whether it's an accounting error, a result of the pandemic, bad economy, poor management, whatever. It takes GOD to heal the land.

About the Author

I started as a Cooperative Education business major at DuVal Senior High School. I worked as a bookkeeper at the Citizen Bank of Maryland during my senior high school year. After I graduated from DuVal, I attended Prince George's Community College, where I received an Associate Arts Degree in Accounting. This degree was useful in private industries and government jobs. In 1977, I took the government entrance examination, scoring 105 when only 70 points were needed for a position. The Federal Government reached out to me regarding job opportunities within the government.

My first job with the Federal Government was aiding FBI agents and Administrative Law Judges with Dishonorable Soldiers' Court Cases. Later, I became an Advocate for Social Security, SSI, and Medicare beneficiaries with the Social Security Administration. Currently, I am a certified minority business owner of one of the largest certified minority-owned waste management businesses in the United States of America.

In 2024, I proudly graduated with a B.S. Degree in General Studies, with a minor in Business Administration, marking another significant milestone in my educational journey.

Imagine a journey of hard work, dedication, and determination that has led to a fulfilling career in government service and ownership of a thriving business. As a powerful advocate for Social Security beneficiaries, I easily interpreted complex laws and regulations, ensuring those in need received the help they deserved. After years of public service, I took my talents into the private sector, becoming a certified minority business owner that serves the D.C. and Metropolitan Illustrious community.

Step into the world filled with challenges, struggles, and triumphs—and be inspired by the incredible journey of an exceptional woman.

Printed by Libri Plureos GmbH in Hamburg, Germany